50 THINGS TO KNOW ABOUT BIRDS IN THE USA

If you know someone who loves birds, I cannot imagine them not learning or enjoying this book.

This book is perfect for both experienced birders and beginners alike. It is written in readable prose and studded with personal stories from the author's many years of observing birds.

50 Things to Know About Birds in Pennsylvania: Birding in the Keystone State
Author Darryl & Jackie Speicher

I really enjoyed this book. I live in the Badger state and I learned a lot of things I didn't know before. The author got me excited about taking up bird watching. Definitely going to plan a day trip to Horicon Marsh.

50 Things to Know About Birds in Wisconsin : Birding in the Badger State
Author Carly Lincoln

D1360509

50 THINGS TO KNOW ABOUT BIRDS IN NEW JERSEY

Birding in the Garden State

Jenilee Jankowski

Cover designed by: Ivana Stamenkovic
Cover Image: pixabay

CZYK Publishing Since 2011.
CZYKPublishing.com
50 Things to Know

Lock Haven, PA
All rights reserved.
ISBN: 9798465066549

50 THINGS TO KNOW
ABOUT BIRDS
IN NEW JERSEY

BOOK DESCRIPTION

Are you travelling to New Jersey soon and want to learn more about the birds you can find in the Garden State? Are you wondering about the species of birds you can find in all the different habitats of New Jersey? Or are you a resident of New Jersey looking to learn more about the birds in your backyard?

If you answered yes to any of these questions, then this book is for you.

50 Things to Know About Birds in New Jersey by author Jenilee Jankowski offers an approach to learning about identifying the birds around the Garden State, while also providing interesting and fun facts about the species described. Most books on birds tell you how to identify birds and where to look for them but can be a bit formal and scientific. Although there is nothing wrong with that, not everyone is well-versed in birding lingo and are looking to learn the basics about the many species that can be seen in New Jersey. Based on knowledge from the world's leading experts you will be privy to information that will enhance your experience of birdwatching in the Garden State.

In these pages you'll discover how to identify males and females of each species, their primary habitat, diet, and nesting habits. This book will help you learn about the birds you can find just by walking outside or where to go to look for a particular species.

By the time you finish this book, you will know everything you need to know about some of the most common birds in the Garden State. So grab YOUR copy today. You'll be glad you did.

TABLE OF CONTENTS

DEDICATION

This book is dedicated to those with a passion for birdwatching.

ABOUT THE AUTHOR

Born and raised in the Garden State, Jenilee has always had a passion for wildlife, especially the species found right where she grew up. She has spent time in all of the habitats around the state and has fallen in love with the many species of birds these varied habitats are home to. Jenilee furthered her knowledge of birds while studying Animal Behavior and Conservation on the Graduate level. Her knowledge and passion make her the perfect person to provide a fun and exciting look at the birds of New Jersey.

She is currently enjoying creating a thriving backyard habitat for as many beautiful birds as possible.

Find her on Amazon Authors!

INTRODUCTION

*"If birds can glide for long periods of time,
then why can't I?"*

-Orville Wright

New Jersey, also known as the Garden State, is unique because there are so many varied types of habitats found here. The Jersey Shore might be the most known place in the state. The coastline is roughly 130 miles long. However, if you add in all of the tidal inlets and marshlands, the National Oceanic and Atmospheric Administration (NOAA) reports over 1,700 miles of coastline in the state. The western part of the state borders the Delaware River, providing yet another unique habitat in the state. The coastline, saltwater marshes, rivers, lakes, and freshwater marshes provide homes to so many beautiful birds.

In addition to this, the Garden State has highly urban areas, such as the northeast corner of the state right outside New York City, gorgeous suburbs, farmlands, and even some countryside areas. Many gorgeous species share our backyards and live right alongside the residents of these areas. The southern part of the state is home to the Pinelands National Reserve, over one million acres of forests, wetlands, and farms. In 1978, the Pinelands National Reserve was the first ever Reserve designated by the United States Congress.

While not really known for its mountains, New Jersey has quite a few mountainous areas. After all, the Appalachian Trail runs for 73 miles through the northwest corner of the state. The mountains and highlands provide another varied type of habitat for the avian residents of the state.

There have been approximately 485 different species of birds identified in New Jersey. Of this number, around 300 are commonly seen, while some are quite rare. Other species spend only one season visiting the Garden State and others only migrate through the state. Many of the species that will be described enjoy living in several different types of habitats. This book is organized into the different types of habitats just described, making it easy for you to determine what kinds of species of birds you will find no matter where you are in the state. The final section is devoted to the amazing raptors that call the Garden State home.

OUR SUBURBAN BACKYARDS

1. AMERICAN GOLDFINCH

This little beauty is the State Bird of New Jersey. They can be found in our backyards, fields, and plains. The males are bright yellow with black wings and a black patch on their heads during the breeding season. The females also turn yellow during the breeding season, but like most bird species, they do not become as bright as the males. During non-breeding seasons, the yellow feathers of both males and females turn a brownish color. The American Goldfinch is the only finch species that molt twice a year. The American Goldfinch will visit bird feeders, as their primary diet includes seeds. Unlike most other bird species, these birds are strictly vegetarians and will not seek out insects as a food source. They are often found flying in flocks, which is an amazing sight to behold. American Goldfinches build nests of grass and stems, usually in bushes, and the females lay two to seven pale blue eggs. In the wintertime, the American Goldfinch will dig burrows into the snow to help keep them warm!

2. NORTHERN CARDINAL

Everyone knows this beautiful bright red bird. Those are the males of the species. The females tend to be a lighter reddish-brown color, and both males and females maintain their colors year-round. Very rarely, a bright yellow Northern Cardinal is spotted, resulting from a lack of red pigment that typically makes the males their well-known bright red color. If you see a yellow Cardinal, consider yourself incredibly lucky! Northern Cardinals can be found in our backyards, thickets, and woodlands of the state. Both male and female Northern Cardinals sing, which is unique, as females of many species leave the singing to the males. They eat seeds, grains, fruit, and insects, and can be spotted on our backyard bird feeders. Cardinals are one of the first birds that will come to a bird feeder in the morning and one of the last species to stop by for an evening snack! When looking for a mate, the male and female Cardinals can be seen touching beaks, almost like they are kissing. Cardinals build nests of twigs and grass in a bush, and each pair can have up to three nests each season. The females will lay three to four eggs. Males can become aggressive when defending their breeding territories.

3. AMERICAN ROBIN

Robins are another easily identifiable bird we can find in our backyards. The American Robin is one of the most common birds in North America. They can be found living in woodlands, farmlands, and fields. Males and females have grey backs and tails with a rusty orange chest. Robins typically eat insects and worms, so they don't usually visit birdfeeders. On an average day, a Robin can eat approximately 14 feet of earthworms! Their keen senses of sight and sound allow them to easily find earthworms. The American Robin can be heard during the early morning hours, helping to prove that the early bird really does get the worm. They are one of the first species we can hear singing in the springtime. Males will sing to attract females and to defend their territory. Robins will build nests of twigs, grass, and mud in a tree or a bush, or even on a window ledge. Females will lay three to five pretty blue eggs two or three times each season. Pigments in their blood and bile make the gorgeous blue color of the eggs. The American Robin has been observed getting drunk by eating fermenting fruit off the ground during the fall and winter when there aren't earthworms readily available for them to enjoy.

4. BLUE JAY

Blue Jays are commonly found in our backyards in the suburbs and also live in forests. They are quickly identified by their bright blue head, back and wings, the black stripes on their wings and tails, their lovely white face, chest, and belly, and their blue head crest. Although we perceive Blue Jays to appear blue, their feathers are not blue from a pigment. They appear blue to us because their feathers only reflect the color blue; it's called light scattering! Test it out for yourself if you find a Blue Jay feather. Just put it in water to disturb the light reflection and the feather will be brown. Blue Jays eat nuts, seeds, fruit, and insects. They will visit our bird feeders. These birds have a very loud call and the males can be aggressive when it comes to breeding season. Blue Jays also serve as an alarm system for other birds in the area. They can imitate the calls of predatory birds, like hawks, and they do this when they see a predator coming around. This alerts the other birds in the area of the danger coming and gives them time to fly away before the predator gets there. However, they have also been observed doing this when there is no predator around in order to get other birds to leave the area so the Blue Jays can have the food all to themselves! Blue Jays build a nest of twigs, grass, and mud. Females will lay two to seven bluish-brown eggs with brown spots. The oldest known Blue Jay lived to be almost 27 years old!

5. BALTIMORE ORIOLE

Another well-known species, the Baltimore Oriole has an orange chest and belly, black head and back, and their wings are black and white with some orange. As with many species, the males are brighter in color while the females are not as brightly colored. These Orioles live in our backyards, parks, orchards, and woodlands. They feed on insects, fruit, and nectar. You won't find an Oriole at a bird feeder, unless you are offering sugar water or grape jelly. The Baltimore Oriole is known to have a sweet tooth! Another favorite food of theirs is grasshoppers. Like the Northern Cardinals, both male and female Baltimore Orioles can be heard singing. They build a really unique, sock-like, hanging nest made of fibers. It can take them almost two weeks to build their nest. Females will lay three to seven pale grey eggs with spots that can be brown, purple, or black.

6. RED-BELLIED WOODPECKER

Woodpeckers are often heard pecking long before they are seen. In New Jersey, there have been 10 different species of Woodpeckers identified, three of which are rare to see. Red-bellied woodpeckers can be heard pecking on the trees in our backyards, parks, on our houses, and local woods and forests. Despite their name, Red-bellied Woodpeckers have a white chest, a red head, and black and white striped backs. Females have a duller red head color than the males. These Woodpeckers eat insects they find in trees and can sometimes be seen visiting a bird feeder. They also enjoy nuts, acorns, and pinecones. The Red-bellied Woodpecker uses its tongue, which is two inches long, and its sticky saliva to grab insects out of the holes they find or peck. Pecking is not only used for finding food, but also for creating a nest site in a tree, finding a mate, and establishing their territory. Red-bellied Woodpeckers nest in existing tree holes or will create their own holes. The females two to six white eggs and the hatchlings are completely helpless once born.

7. AMERICAN CROW

This all-black bird can be found in most parts of the state, including our backyards, cities, farms, marshes, fields, and woodlands. They are a very common sight around the Garden State. When the sun shines on these birds, they have a purplish shine to their feathers. American Crows have a very distinct caw that most of us can probably identify. Crows will eat pretty much anything including plants, fruit, eggs, insects, frogs, fish, and they even scavenge dead animals. These birds create nests of twigs and branches in trees and the females lay three to six bluish-green eggs that can have brown and grey blotches on one end. Crows can have a bad reputation, but they are incredibly intelligent. Crows are known to make tools, such as using a hook-shaped twig to help them pull grubs out of tight spaces. They can learn the patterns and behaviors of humans in the neighborhoods where they live, such as learning the garbage truck route so they can scavenge food. American Crows can recognize individual humans and will learn which humans will feed them and which will not. Researchers have found that Crows have 'funerals' for their deceased flock members.

8. RUBY-THROATED HUMMINGBIRD

Hummingbirds are one of the most beloved species of birds. New Jersey is regularly home to two species of hummingbirds, one of which is the Ruby-throated Hummingbird. This species can be found in backyards, gardens, and forests. The males have males have a green head and back, pale chest and belly, and a bright red throat. The females are slightly duller and have a white throat. They feed on nectar from tubular flowers and will drink from feeders. Just boil water and sugar, let it cool, and put it in a feeder to attract these spectacular birds and watch them hover while feeding. They can consume up to twice their body weight in one day! Their wings beat at over 50 times per second! The heartbeat of a Ruby-throated Hummingbird can reach up to 1,200 beats per minute, with the average being around 600 beats per minute. In comparison, the average human heartbeat is about 70 beats per minute. This species builds nests of plant matter, moss, and spider webs on tree branches. The females will lay one to three tiny white eggs.

9. NORTHERN MOCKINGBIRD

These birds are found mostly in suburban areas around the state. They are predominantly grey and black but have white chests and white feathers on their wings. Northern Mockingbirds eat berries and insects. They are very territorial birds. They will dive at anything, even people, to protect their nest sites and feeding grounds. Both males and females of this species can be heard singing almost nonstop. They are extremely skilled at mimicking the calls of other bird species and even other animals like frogs and toads, hence the name 'Mockingbird.' The Northern Mockingbird can also mimic the sounds of machinery and music. The Northern Mockingbird has been an inspiration in pop culture, from the famous novel To Kill a Mockingbird to the Hunger Games franchise's Mockingjay. They make nests in trees using twigs, leaves, and grass. Females lay two to six pale blue eggs with reddish brown spots. One Northern Mockingbird female set a record by laying 27 eggs in a single breeding season!

15

10. BARN SWALLOW

These cute little birds can be found in our backyards, in fields, on beaches, and near other bodies of water. Barn Swallows can be found living on every continent except Antarctica. They have blue backs and brown bellies with grey wings. They eat flies, beetles, bees, and moths. Barn Swallows mostly feed while they are flying. Their nests are made of mud on the sides of houses or other buildings. It can take over 1,000 trips to gather the supplies needed to build their nests. Because it such a long and arduous process, Barn Swallows will take over an unused nest if they can find one. The females lay three to seven light pink eggs with spots. The males tend to be aggressive toward other males during the breeding season. Barn Swallows will also dive at humans and other animals if they feel you are too close to their nests, and they even make a special alarm call. There have been nine species of swallows identified in New Jersey, two of which are rare.

11. COMMON NIGHTHAWK

Common Nighthawks live in woodlands, fields, the suburbs, and in cities. They are a mottled brown, black, and grey with a white stripe near the tips of their wings. Despite their name, Common Nighthawks are not related to hawks, and are actually related to Whip-poor-wills. As their name suggests, Common Nighthawks are mostly nocturnal and can be difficult to spot during the day. Because of their erratic flying behavior to catch their prey at dusk, the Common Nighthawk can be easily mistaken for bats. These birds typically eat insects. They can eat up to 500 mosquitoes in a night! Common Nighthawks have very interesting courtship rituals. The male Nighthawk will fly high up into the sky and then dive straight down in an effort to catch a female's attention. Once they find a mate, they do not build nests. Females will lay one to three eggs on the ground. During the wintertime, the Common Nighthawk will migrate south to warmer weather in large flocks.

12. SONG SPARROW

There are more than 25 species of sparrows in New Jersey. One of the most common species that can be found in the suburbs, wetlands, and woodlands is the Song Sparrow. They are also one of the most recognizable species. Song Sparrows are grey and brown with white chests. They eat seeds and insects and are frequently spotted enjoying backyard bird feeders. They can be pretty aggressive around bird feeders, even chasing off species that are much larger than they are. These birds will build nests using grasses and twigs in trees or bushes. Females will lay one to seven eggs that are bluish-green with brown, reddish, or lilac spots. If the first brood of eggs does not survive, the female will try up to seven times in a season to produce a viable brood. As their name suggests, male Song Sparrows sing frequently and will do so for mating and defending their territory. Males can perform up to 20 different melodies. Researchers have discovered that the Song Sparrow can sing over 2,300 individual songs in one day!

13. MOURNING DOVE

This is one of seven species of pigeons and doves found in New Jersey. Unfortunately, Mourning Doves are one of the most frequently hunted bird species in North America. They can be found in fields, woodlands, farmland, the suburbs, and cities. Mourning Doves are grey or tan with black spots on their wings and have white on parts of their tail feathers and spots beneath each eye. They eat worms and seeds. Their nests are built in trees or bushes and are made of twigs, pine needles, and grass. The females will lay two white eggs. Mourning Doves mate for life, and both parents help care for the babies. Males and females of this species both make calls. But their most distinctive and well-known noise is the whistling or whinnying sound made by their wings when take flight. Mourning Doves are fast birds and can reach speeds of up to 55 miles per hour! These birds are also known as Turtle Doves, like in the classic Christmas song.

14. RED-WINGED BLACKBIRD

The Red-winged Blackbird is absolutely gorgeous, and a personal favorite. While females are a mottled brown and white color with small patches of rust-color on their wings and necks, the males are simply spectacular. They are fully black with bright red and yellow shoulder patches These birds are found in the suburbs, fields, marshes, and wetlands. They are one of the most populous bird species in the entirety of North America. These birds are one of the first to announce the arrival of spring with their songs and can be heard in the early morning hours. They eat insects, seeds, and grains. They typically roost in flocks. Males are highly territorial during the breeding season and will chase away other birds and attack predators. Unlike the Mourning Doves, the Red-winged Blackbird does not mate for life, a male can have up to 15 mates! The Red-winged Blackbirds' nests are built of mud and grass and the females will lay three to five blue-green eggs.

15. TUFTED TITMOUSE

These birds can be found in backyards but are more common in forests and swamps. They are mostly grey, but have a white chest and rusty orange spots on their sides. They also have a grey head crest, making them relatively easy to identify. The Tufted Titmouse eats insects and seeds, and can be observed at bird feeders. Tree holes are home to their nests, which are built out of leaves, grass, bark, and sometimes hair or fur. The females will lay three to nine eggs with reddish spots on them. The male and female will mate for life. These are one of the birds that do not migrate, so they can be seen in New Jersey all year long. The Tufted Titmouse has a high whistling song. In Cherokee legend, the Tufted Titmouse is seen as a messenger.

https://en.wikipedia.org/wiki/File:Sturnella_magna_-Mexico-8.jpg

16. EASTERN MEADOWLARK

While the Eastern Meadowlark can be seen in suburban backyards, it is more likely to find this species on farmlands and areas that are more open and grassier than some suburbs. Unfortunately, because of urbanization and loss of habitat, the population of the Eastern Meadowlark has been declining since the 1960s. Conserving farmlands and grassy fields will be essential to keeping the population healthy. The Eastern Meadowlark has yellow belly and throat, a brown and white mottled back, and a black V-shaped ring around their neck, giving them the appearance of wearing a necklace. This species eats crickets, grasshoppers, caterpillars, and grubs. They build their nests on the ground using grass, stems, and bark. The females will lay two to seven white eggs. During the breeding season, the males are very vocal and can be heard singing throughout the day.

PONDS AND LAKES

17. CANADA GOOSE

New Jersey is home to more than 45 species of geese, ducks, and other waterfowl. By far the most common and recognizable goose species is the Canada Goose. These geese can be found in cities, suburbs, parks, and fields. They have a brownish body with a long black neck and head with white patches on their face. The Canada Goose is the largest goose species in the world. They are typically found in flocks and are seen flying in the classic V-shape. The Canada Goose does not sing but instead makes a honking noise and even hisses when feeling threatened. Canada Geese eat plants, berries, seeds, and grains. They build nests made of grass, moss, and their own down feathers near a water source. The females will lay two to eight white eggs. At only one day old, a gosling can dive up to 40 feet underwater!

18. WOOD DUCK

Wood Ducks live near wooded rivers and ponds, and in swamps and marshes. The males are several shades and patterns of brown and white one their bodies. They have shiny green heads with purple patches and red rings around their eyes. They have blue patches on their wing and the males have longer feathers on the backs of their heads. This is one of the most colorful species of waterfowl. Females are brown and white, and have darker blue patches on their wings. The females' head feathers are not as long as the males. They eat plants, seeds, fruits, and insects Wood Ducks make their nests tree holes using with their own down. Females will lay 6 to 15 cream-colored eggs. If a female cannot find a good nest site, she will simply lay her eggs in another Wood Duck's nest, even if there are already eggs in it! They have also been known to use abandoned Woodpecker nests. Interestingly, the Wood Duck will mate with other duck species, such as Mallards, and create hybrid species. Another name for Wood Ducks is Carolina Ducks.

19. MALLARD DUCK

Mallard Ducks are found living near ponds, lakes, and in marshes. Similar to Wood Ducks, the males are much more colorful than the females. A female Mallard Duck has mottled brown and white feathers. The males have brown bodies with an emerald green head and blue patches on their wings. Mallard Ducks eat water plants, insects, seeds, and acorns. They will scratch a depression into the ground and line it with grass and their own down feathers. The females will lay one to 13 greenish-tan eggs. Mallard Ducks are often found living in harmony with Canada Geese, Wood Ducks, and other goose, duck, and waterfowl species. Mallard Ducks can be bred to be domesticated. Mallard Ducks can fly at speeds of up to 70 miles per hour and can take off from the water nearly vertically!

20. DOUBLE-CRESTED CORMORANT

Only three species of cormorants have been seen in New Jersey, including the Double-crested Cormorant. These birds require large ponds or lakes, as their main diet is fish. They will also eat some crustaceans and insects. Cormorants are known for their ability to dive underwater and chase their prey. Double-crested Cormorants have black feathers with orange skin near their eyes. During mating season, males will open their mouths to show off the blue skin inside to attract a female. They live in and build their nests in colonies. They use sticks, seaweed, and grass on the ground, on rocks, or even in trees. The females will lay one to seven light blue eggs. The Double-crested Cormorant, and other Cormorant species, can be seen perched on trees or rocks with their wings open. They do this after diving to allow their feathers to dry out. Unlike other waterfowl species, Cormorant feathers are not fully waterproof. By having feathers that absorb water, they are able to be more efficient divers. This comes at a cost, though, as they are not very good at flying and it uses up a lot of their energy.

MARSHES AND ESTUARIES

21. GREATER YELLOWLEGS

This species is found in marshes. They have a brown and white back, white belly, black bill, and as their name suggests, yellow legs. They will eat invertebrates, small frogs, and fish. They are active hunters and can be seen running along the shoreline trying to catch their prey. Greater Yellowlegs nest on the ground by making a small depression in the moss near the base of a tree. The female will lay three to four eggs that are grey or brown. Greater Yellowlegs will wade deeper into the water than other birds that live in this type of habitat. The courtship display is overt and eye-catching. The male will fly up, then dive down while singing. They will then land near the female and run around her in circles. Because they tend to nest in areas that have high populations of bugs and mosquitos, they are one of the least-studied birds living in these kinds of areas.

22. MARSH WREN

There are seven species of Wren found in New Jersey. Males of all species sing loud songs during the breeding season. The Marsh Wren is found in marshes and wetlands. They have brown backs with black on their wings and tail feathers, and a lighter belly. The Marsh Wren is pretty difficult to spot, as they are a secretive species. Even when they are calling, they typically remain hidden. This is another species that can be heard long before it can be seen. The Marsh Wren eats insects and spiders. They build a dome-shaped nest with a hole in the top made of different types of grasses. The female will lay three to ten brown eggs. The males can learn to imitate the songs of other species, and have been found to be able to imitate songs played off a tape recorder by researchers.

23. AMERICAN COOT

The American Coot, or the Mud Hen, lives near lakes and ponds, and in marshes and estuaries. They are dark grey with a white patch under their tail. They have a white bill with red at the base. They have large feet that look too big for their bodies. American Coots eat small fish, tadpoles, snails, crayfish, insects, and water plants. This species can be quite lazy and when they don't feel like hunting, they will steal food from other birds. They build their nests hidden in vegetation on the edge of the water. The female will lay up to ten pink eggs with brown spots. This is one of ten similar species found in New Jersey. The oldest known American Coot was 22 years old.

24. SANDHILL CRANE

The Sandhill Crane is the only Crane species found in New Jersey. They live in the wetlands and marshes. Sandhill Cranes have long necks and long legs. They have a red and white face, a long dark beak, a greyish-yellow body, and a large tuft of tail feathers. These birds can stand up to four feet tall and their wingspans can be up to seven feet wide. They eat seeds, insects, snails, frogs, and lizards. They build nests of plant matter that float on the surface of the water. The female will lay one to three light brown eggs. Sandhill Cranes make a buzzing call. This species migrates south in the winter months. A fossil of a Sandhill Crane was found in Florida that is estimated to be 2.5 million years old. These birds have been around for a very long time!

25. SNOWY EGRET

New Jersey is home to 14 egret and heron species. The Snowy Egret lives in salt marshes, mud flats, swamps, ponds, lakes, and river estuaries. They are all white with a long thin neck, a thin black beak that turns yellow near the eyes, and they have long black legs with yellow feet. During the breeding season, males and females grow long curved feathers. They are shorter than the Sandhill Crane, reaching only about two feet tall. Females are typically shorter than males. They eat fish but also small animals like snails, frogs, lizards, snakes, worms, and insects. They build a nest of sticks and grasses in colonies that are typically found on the outer branches of trees and shrubs. The female will lay two to six pale green eggs. Males engage in a courtship dance to attract a mate. A male and female will only recognize each other after performing an elaborate ritual, even after they have laid their eggs! The breeding season feathers of the Snowy Egret were used on women's hats in the late 1800s, almost leading to their extinction in the early 1900s. Thankfully, the trend ended and the population of these beautiful birds was able to rebound.

26. GREAT BLUE HERON

The Great Blue Heron can be found in almost every part of the United States. They live year-round in New Jersey. They live in marshes, lakes, and ponds, and can live in either fresh or saltwater. The Great Blue Heron, as its name suggests, has a greyish-blue body, a white and black head with orange bill, and longer dark feathers coming off the back of their head. The Great Blue Heron stands at three to four and a half feet tall and have massive wingspans reaching up to six and a half feet long. The Great Blue Heron eats fish, amphibians, reptiles, small mammals, insects, and other birds. They will wade into the water and stand very still while waiting for their prey to come to them. One of their hunting techniques is to use their bills to impale fish. The Great Blue Herons have feathers on their chests that continue to grow throughout their lives. They use these feathers like a washcloth to wipe off fish slime and other oils and slimes found in the waters where they live. Great Blue Herons will build a nest of sticks in trees, bushes, or on the ground. They nest in colonies of up to 500 pairs of Herons. The female will lay two to six pale blue eggs. Males and females take turns incubating their eggs.

THE COASTLINE

27. GULLS

The quintessential birds of the Jersey Shore, there are over 35 species of gulls and terns in New Jersey. Two of the most common gull species are the Laughing Gull and the Great Black-backed Gull. Gulls live in coastal areas. Most species are different patterns of grey and white, typically having white bodies and grey wings and heads. live on the coast. The younger gulls of most species have more brown and tan in their plumage. They have loud, squawking calls and can be heard calling while scavenging on the beach and dive-bombing beachgoers for their snacks. Most gull species nest on the ground using vegetation. The females will lay around two or three eggs, with the color varying from species to species. The majority of gull species mate for life.

28. COMMON TERN

Just like gulls, Common Terns are found along the beaches and are typically seen with gulls. The Common Tern has a white belly, grey wings, a darker head, and red-orange feet and bill. They eat small fish, crustaceans, squid, and insects. The Common Tern scrapes a depression into the ground and then lines it with vegetation, bones, and stones. Females will lay one to four olive-colored eggs with brown splotches. Like many birds that live along the ocean, the Common Tern does not drink fresh water. They are able to drink saltwater thanks to special nasal glands that excrete the salt. Common Terns are also known as the Sea Swallow. A group of Common Terns is called a "committee."

29. AMERICAN OYSTERCATCHER

The American Oystercatcher is the only species of Oystercatcher found in New Jersey. It is found along the coastline. They have reddish-yellow eyes, a reddish-orange bill, a white belly, a brown back, and a black head. As its name suggests, they eat mollusks such as oysters, clams, and mussels. The American Oystercatcher is able to dive and swim underwater to catch their prey and to get away from predators. They build a nest within or behind the dunes by making a depression in the sand and lining it with vegetation. The female will lay two to four gray and brown eggs. The males will make a piping call during mating season. Both males and females will become aggressive when defending their breeding territory. The American Oystercatcher was originally known as the "Sea Pie," but its name was changed in 1731 after a naturalist observed the bird eating oysters.

30. PIPING PLOVER

There are ten Plover species found in New Jersey. The Piping Plover has a white belly and neck, a sand-colored back, either a black or white ring around its neck, and orange legs. They live along the coastline. Piping Plovers will eat worms, snails, small crustaceans, and insects such as flies and beetles. When looking for food, the Piping Plover will sometimes stick one foot out into wet sand and shake it really quickly in an effort to disturb its prey and make it easier to catch. This technique is called "foot-trembling." They will nest in the sand above the high tide line by digging a depression into the sand, sometimes lining it with shells or pebbles. They lay two to four white eggs with brownish black spots. Piping Plovers can be seeing running quickly along the beach and making a piping noise, as their name suggests.

31. SANDERLING

There are approximately 40 species of sandpipers and related birds that call the Garden State home, including the Sanderling. They living along the coastline. They have black legs and a black bill, a white belly, and a light brown back. Sanderlings eat aquatic invertebrates such as small crabs, worms, mollusks, and horseshoe crab eggs. They build a nest of leaves, moss, and twigs on the ground. The females lay three to four eggs that are greenish-brown or greenish blue with brown spots. Sanderlings are best known for running along the surf and chasing the waves at the Jersey Shore. They do not have a hind toe, like other sandpiper species, which allows them to be strong and efficient runners. This species can be found on every continent except Antarctica. They breed in the Arctic and spend their winters along the coasts.

32. DUNLIN

The Dunlin is another species of sandpiper. They live in coastal areas and estuaries. These have orange and brown backs with a lighter-colored chest when breeding. When it is not breeding season, the orange fades away and their bellies turn black. Dunlins have black legs and a long black curved bill. Female Dunlins have longer bills than male Dunlins. They eat worms, beetles, snails, small clams, spiders, and flies. They nest by scraping a depression into the ground near grassy areas. The female will lay three to four olive or brownish colored eggs. Males and females take turns incubating the eggs. But after the eggs hatch, the female abandons the brood and leaves the male to take care of the babies. Dunlins are territorial and will chase other birds away while making a loud trilling sound.

THE PINELANDS AND OTHER WOODLANDS

33. CHICKADEE

Chickadees are found in forests, parks, and thickets. They have a white belly, grey, white, and black wings, a grey back, and black throat and head with a white stripe. Chickadees eat berries, seeds, and insects. They can be seen at bird feeders in rural parts of the state. During the wintertime, Chickadees need to eat 20 times more food than they need in the summer! They will nest in a nest box, small natural cavities, or dig their own holes. They build a nest with moss inside their chosen hole. Chickadees will lay one to thirteen white eggs with reddish brown dots. They live in flocks. Within each flock, there are many calls the birds use to communicate with each other. The different calls have been compared to the words of human languages.

34. WILD TURKEY

Wild Turkeys are mostly found in woodlands but are also frequently seen in the suburbs. Wild Turkey females are large brown birds with grey featherless heads and red necks with a flap of red skin. Males are much larger, have more colorful feathers on their bodies, and have larger tail feathers that form a fan shape. Males have red and blue featherless faces and their necks have bumpy loose skin called a wattle. They eat fruit, seeds, acorns, and insects. Females lay four to 17 white eggs with reddish spots in a little depression on the ground. Wild Turkeys can be found in flocks reaching up to 200 individuals in the wintertime. Wild Turkeys make the same gobbling noise we all associate with Turkeys. A town in Bergen County, Paramus, which you may have heard of because it is famous for its malls and Blue Laws, got its name from the Lenni Lenape Native American word for "land of the wild turkeys."

35. TURKEY VULTURE

The Turkey Vulture lives in open areas with trees and can be found in the suburbs. They are dark brown or black with a featherless red head. Having a featherless head allows them to keep their heads clean when eating carrion, or dead animals. When seeing them flying, the underside of their wings looks grey and black. The wingspan of a Turkey Vulture can be up to six feet long, but they only weigh about two to four pounds! They are surprisingly lightweight for such a large bird. Turkey Vultures will eat insects, small animals, and sometimes fruit, but they are best known for eating carrion. Their keen sense of smell allows them to detect carrion from over a mile away. Turkey Vultures do not build a nest, and instead the female will lay one to three white eggs with dark spots in a cave, on rocks, or in a hollow log. Turkey Vultures can often be seen in the early morning hours standing in the sun with their wings spread open, like a Double-crested Cormorant. The Turkey Vulture does this to increase their body temperature after a cool night.

36. RUFFED GROUSE

The Ruffed Grouse lives in forests. They have dark gray or brown backs and lighter chests. Their tail is fan shaped and striped. Ruffed Grouse spend most of their time on the ground. They eat leaves, nuts, fruit, insects, and tree buds. They make their nests in dead leaves next to a tree or rock. Females will lay seven to 16 light brown eggs. Ruffed Grouse are relatively quiet but will make a squealing or hissing sound when frightened or threatened. Mothers will also make a cooing hum to their babies. The Ruffed Grouse is also known as a "Drummer" or a "Thunder Chicken." The name "Drummer" comes from their courtship display, which involves making a drumming sound by rapidly beating their wings, creating a low frequency sound that can be heard up to 25 miles away. During the wintertime, the Ruffed Grouse will burrow themselves in the snow to keep warm, stay out of the wind, and protect themselves from predators.

37. EASTERN WHIP-POOR-WILL

The Eastern Whip-poor-will lives in open woodlands around the state. They are a mottled brown and white with a flat head, and a black face and throat. Their coloring allows them to camouflage with the trees during the day, making them difficult to spot. They are mostly nocturnal and sing at dusk. These birds are named after their song, as the call they make sounds like 'whip-poor-will.' One Eastern Whip-poor-will was recorded making over 1,000 calls in a row! They are difficult to find and are more often heard than seen. They eat moths and insects. Eastern Whip-poor-wills do not make nests. Females will lay two cream-colored spotted eggs directly onto the leaf litter. During the wintertime, the Eastern Whip-poor-will flies south to warmer weather.

38. PINE WARBLER

New Jersey is home to approximately 40 species of Warblers. The Pine Warbler makes its home in the pine forests of the state. It is rare to find this bird living anywhere other than pine forests. They are mostly yellow with white and brown wings and tail feathers, and a white or grey underside. Pine Warblers eat caterpillars, beetles, ants, bees, spiders, fruits, and seeds. They build their nests in pine trees using grass, bark, twigs, and use spider or caterpillar silk to hold the nests together. Females will lay three to five white or grey eggs with brown speckles. Males are aggressive during breeding season. The Pine Warbler serenades the forest with its steady, musical song. A group of Pine Warblers is called a "cone," like a pinecone! Researchers estimate the population of Pine Warblers to be around 11 million birds.

39. PRAIRIE WARBLER

Another common species of Warbler found in New Jersey is the
Prairie Warbler. Despite its name, it lives in forests as well as fields.
They have a yellow head and body with black stripes on their sides
and head, and grey and brown wings and tail. Prairie Warblers eat
insects and spiders. They build nests in trees or shrubs using grass,
moss and feathers. Females lay three to five brown or grey spotted
eggs. Females will eat the egg shells after the babies hatch. Male
Prairie Warblers have two songs, one they sing during courtship and
another they sing to defend their territory.

40. YELLOW-THROATED VIREO

The Yellow-throated Vireo lives in the woodlands of the state. They have a yellow head and chest, and belly, and grey wings. Yellow-throated Vireos look like they are wearing glasses due to a yellow ring around their eyes. They eat spiders, butterflies, beetles, bees, moths, stinkbugs, and sometimes fruits and seeds. A male will find several different potential nest sites. He will show these to the female, who will then make the final decision for the location of the nest. They then build their nest in tree using bark, grasses, and leaves held together with spiderwebs. The nest is cup shaped and is suspended from a branch, similar to the Baltimore Orioles's nest. he female will lay three to five white eggs with dark spots. Courtship involves males swaying side to side while singing to attract a female.

41. WOOD THRUSH

There are 11 species of Thrush living in New Jersey, three of which are rare. One of the more common species is the Wood Thrush. This species lives in forests and woodlands. They have a white and black spotted belly, a brown back, and a yellowish neck. Wood Thrush eat beetles, flies, spiders, snails, and fruits. They weave their nests using grass, leaves, and stems. Females lay three to four turquoise eggs. Males will sing all day to attract females. Unfortunately, the number of Wood Thrush in New Jersey is declining. The Wood Thrush has been observed engaging in a behavior called "anting" during which the bird will hold ants in its beak and then rub the ants on their feathers. It is unknown for sure why they do this, but researchers believe it may allow the birds to use the substance secreted by the ants as a defense mechanism.

42. AMERICAN WOODCOCK

The American Woodcock lives in forests and woodlands but can also be found in fields near urban and suburban areas. They are a mottled brown and black color with a long brown bill. The bill seems almost too long for its body and gives the bird a comical look. The American Woodcock uses its long bill to probe the ground for their favorite food, earthworms. They will also eat ants, spiders, beetles, and flies. An American Woodcock can eat its weight in earthworms in one day. This species does not build a nest but instead forms a depression in leaf litter on the ground. The female will lay one to five greyish orange eggs. During courtship, males will launch themselves into the air while making buzzing and twittering sounds and then diving back to the ground to impress the females. When an American Woodcock is scared, it will freeze, no matter where it is!

RAPTORS AND OWLS

43. GREAT HORNED OWL

New Jersey is home to over 30 species of Owls and Raptors. The Great Horned Owl is one of the most recognizable species thanks to the tufts of feathers on their heads that look like horns or ears. Their bodies are mottled brown and white. They have round faces that are grey or white or light brown, and they have big yellow eyes. The Great Horned Owl can be found in woodlands, swamps, suburbs, and sometimes even parks in cities. They eat small mammals like mice, rabbits, moles, chipmunks, and squirrels. This species usually hunts at night but will hunt during the day at times. Their wings are almost silent when flying, allowing them to sneak up on their prey without being heard. They typically use a nest of sticks built by another species but can use holes in trees, cliff ledges, or deserted buildings. The female will lay one to four white round eggs. They attract their mates by puffing up and bobbing up and down. In addition to the hooting noise we most associate with owls, the Great Horned Owl can also be heard bill-clapping, hissing, and screaming when defending their territory.

44. BARN OWL

The Barn Owl lives in grasslands, marshes, forests, suburbs, and cities. They have a white chest and face with a light brown back and wings. Females are typically larger than males. Barn owls eat small mammals like mice voles, bats, rabbits, some other birds. Unlike the Great Horned Owl, Barn Owls will only hunt at night. They make a nest using their regurgitated pellets, which are the parts of their prey that they cannot digest such as the bones, fur, claws, and teeth. They build these nests in tree holes, and in many man-made structures such as barn lofts, church steeples, houses, and nest boxes. The females will lay two to 18 white eggs that typically become dull and dirty due to the nest material. Barn Owls mate for life. While the average lifespan for Barn Owl is around four years, the oldest known wild Barn Owl lived to be 34 years old! The Barn Owl does not hoot like other owls. Instead, they make a shrieking scream.

45. OSPREY

Ospreys live anywhere they can access water that is home to their primary diet of fish. They can be found on every continent except Antarctica. They have a white belly, throat, and head, and a brown back and wings. They also have brown patches near their eyes. Osprey will dive into the water to get their fish. They typically dive within three feet of the surface. In addition to fish, Osprey will occasionally eat other birds, squirrels, and salamanders. They build nests made of sticks that are lined with bark, grasses, and algae. Their nests can be up to six feet in diameter when it is an established nest that has been used for several years. The female will lay one to four creamy pink eggs with brownish spots. Males and females will aggressively defend their nest area. Ospreys are also known as a "Fish Hawk" or a "Sea Hawk." Their average life span is around 20 years. This species of bird has been around for at least 11 million years!

46. RED-TAILED HAWK

The Red-tailed Hawk is one of the more common species that can be spotted around the state. They live near fields, in woodlands, and around the suburbs. The Red-tailed Hawk has a mottled brown and white back, head, belly, with more white on their belly, under their wings, and their legs. Their tail feathers are a reddish orange color, giving them their name. Their prey includes mice, rabbits, squirrels, and other birds. They build nests of sticks that can be over six feet high and three feet wide on tall trees, window ledges, or billboard platforms. Females lay one to five white eggs with brown speckles. They will aggressively defend their nests and territories. Red-tailed Hawks typically mate for life. They are easy to spot when flying, thanks to their tail feathers, and are frequently seen flying above roadways or perched on poles along roadways.

47. COOPER'S HAWK

The Cooper's Hawk can also be found in the suburbs, parks, fields, and woodlands. They have a mottled white and light brown, almost rusty looking, chest, a white tail, and a grey back and wings. Their tails appear rounded, which helps to identify this species. The Cooper's Hawk feeds mostly on other birds such as Pigeons, Mourning Doves, Robins, Jays, and Chickens. They can sometimes be found watching bird feeders where their prey birds are likely to congregate in large numbers. They will also eat small mammals such as chipmunks and squirrels. They build nests of sticks in trees. The female will lay two to six light blue eggs. The Cooper's Hawk is a very agile flier and a powerful raptor.

48. PEREGRINE FALCON

The Peregrine Falcon can be found in many areas of the state. They live on the coast, in cities, near lakes, and in the mountains. They have a brown and white mottled belly, a white throat and chest, and a dark grey head and back. They eat mostly birds but will sometimes eat bats or steal prey from other raptors. They build their nest on cliffs, bridges, and buildings by scraping a depression into the substrate. The females lay two to five creamy brown eggs that have brown or red or purple spots. The Peregrine Falcon is the world's fastest animal. They can reach speeds of up to 240mph while diving. They can hit their prey so hard in the air that it is stunned or even killed. During the 1960s and 1970s, the population of Peregrine Falcons was down to only 39 pairs due to the extensive use of the pesticide DDT. However, with strict laws and then banning of DDT in 1972, the population has been able to stabilize, and we can enjoy this amazing raptor in the Garden State.

49. BALD EAGLE

The Bald Eagle, as many of know, is the National Emblem of the United States and has been since 1782. There is now a nesting pair of Bald Eagles found in every county of New Jersey. They live near water, as their diet consists mostly of fish. In addition to fish, Bald Eagles will eat birds, reptiles, and amphibians. Bald Eagles have dark brown bodies, white heads and tail feathers, and a yellow beak. They build nests of sticks, grass, and moss on trees. The Bald Eagle builds the largest nest of all bird species. Their nests can reach five to six feet in diameter and two to four feet tall. Females will lay one to three white eggs per season. The male and female take turns incubating the eggs and caring for the babies. They typically mate for life. During their courtship rituals, the male and female will fly to a great height, lock talons, and then drop toward the ground, breaking apart just before reaching the ground.

50. GOLDEN EAGLE

The Golden Eagle is brown with golden feathers on the back of its head and neck. They have dark beaks and yellow feet. They live near mountains, rivers, cliffs, bluffs, grasslands, and forests. The Golden Eagle will eat rabbits, squirrels, and will hunt larger mammals such as deer, swans, and coyotes. Golden Eagles will also scavenge the prey of other predators. They build nests of sticks and vegetation on cliffs or in trees. Their nests can be quite large, reaching five to six feet wide. The largest nest on record was 20 feet tall and eight and a half feet wide! The female lays one to three white or pale pink eggs. Like the Bald Eagle, their courtship rituals are impressive, but not quite as dramatic. The Golden Eagle will repeatedly swoop up and dive back down to impress their potential mate.

A majestic Golden Eagle perched on a tree branch.

OTHER HELPFUL RESOURCES

All About Birds: https://allaboutbirds.org

Bird Watching HQ: https://birdwatchinghq.com

Exploring Nature: https://exploringnature.org

New Jersey Audubon: https://njaudubon.org

New Jersey Pinelands National Reserve:
https://www.nps.gov/pine/index.htm

New Jersey: https://visitnj.org

READ OTHER
50 THINGS TO KNOW ABOUT BIRDS IN THE UNITED STATES BOOKS

50 Things to Know

Stay up to date with new releases on Amazon:

https://amzn.to/2VPNGr7

CZYKPublishing.com

50 Things to Know

We'd love to hear what you think about our content! Please leave your honest review of this book on Amazon and Goodreads. We appreciate your positive and constructive feedback. Thank you.

Made in United States
North Haven, CT
20 April 2022

18429133R00043